Ada's dad was a very famous British poet named Lord Byron. Unfortunately, she never met him. He moved to a different country before she was born in 1815. This means her mother, Lady Byron, had to be a single mother while raising Ada.

INSPIRED INNER GENIUS

Ada Lovelace

Ada Lovelace lived before the invention of cars, phones, and electricity. Despite this, she became one of the earliest computer programmers[1] – 100 years before the first modern computer was even built!

Not many girls went to school or learned how to read at this time. Luckily for Ada, Lady Byron was a smart and independent[2] mom. She was a mathematician, and she made sure that Ada learned as much as she could about science and math.

Ada's childhood was hard. She got sick often and had to stay in bed a lot. When she felt well, she did the things she loved. She enjoyed imagining new inventions, like the flying machine she designed when she was 13. She did very well in math, science, and writing.

Most girls at the time were raised to find good husbands and have children. Being beautiful and polite was more important than learning. In fact, some men did not like it when women were educated. But Lady Byron wanted Ada to be intelligent, talented, and strong on her own.

HE WHITE HORSE

This didn't stop Ada from having the best of both worlds[3]. She knew she could be smart and still find love. When she grew up, she married a man that encouraged her to keep following her dreams. They had three children together.

Ada met someone named Charles Babbage when she was 17. They became lifelong friends. Charles was a professor, inventor, and mathematician. They were passionate[4] about many of the same things, and they loved to talk about math and science.

Charles designed a machine called the Analytical Engine[5]. Its job was to answer difficult math problems. It would be huge! It had 8,000 parts and weighed more than 5 tons. Today, scientists believe the Analytical Engine is the first computer anyone ever thought of.

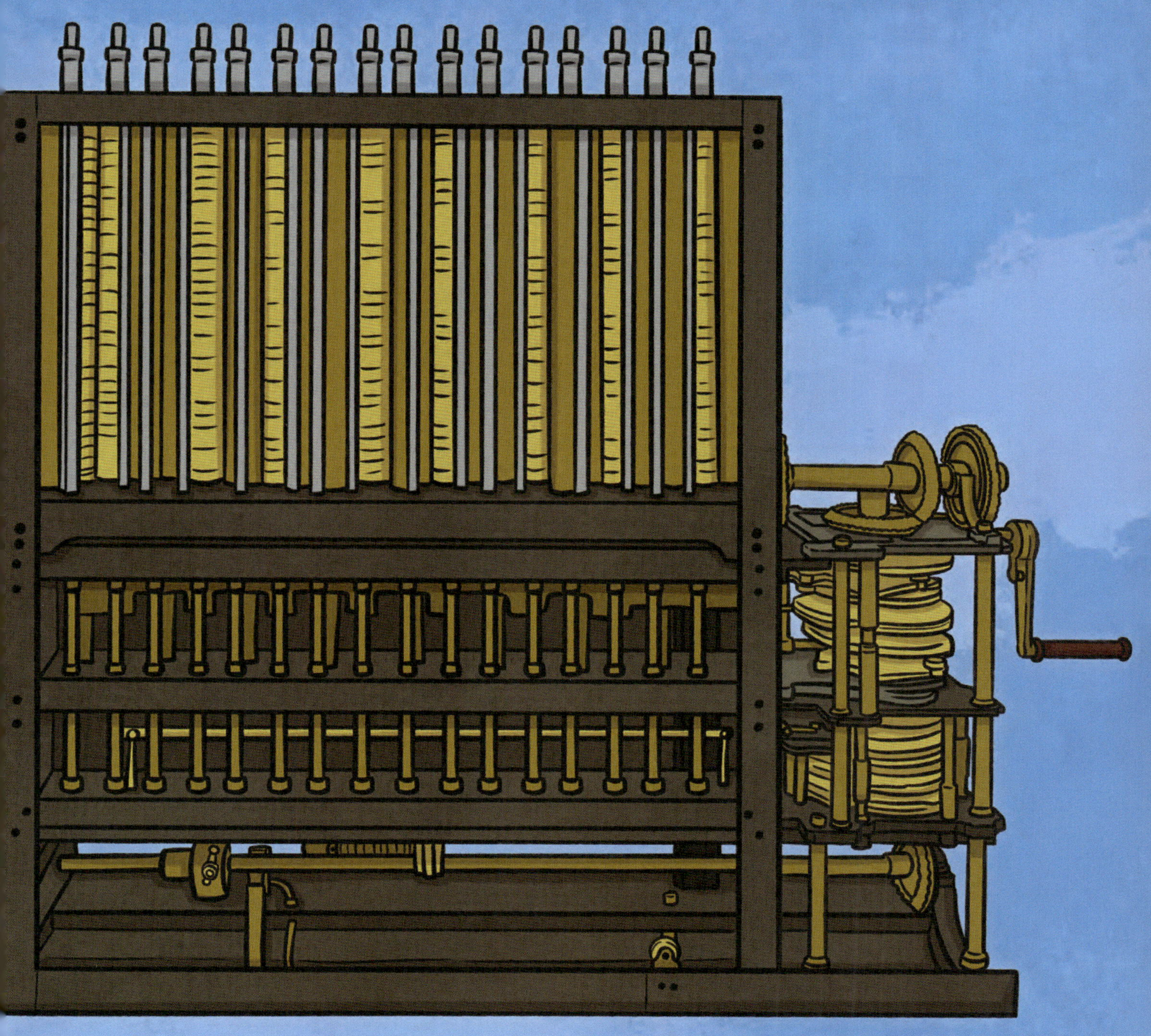

Unfortunately, Charles's ideas were ahead of their time. It was hard getting money to build his machine because most people didn't understand what it could do. Luckily, Ada wasn't like most people. She knew how important the Analytical Engine could be. She also thought of ways to make it even better.

So Charles asked Ada for help. She agreed to translate[6] an article on the Analytical Engine into English. But she didn't stop there. She also added her own notes on the Analytical Engine and how it could be used. In fact, the article was three times longer once she was done with it.

She talked about what the Analytical Engine might someday be able to achieve. People could take numbers and turn them into a unique language that would tell the machine what to do. Amazingly, this is exactly what computer programmers did 100 years later when working with the first computers!

No one realized how revolutionary[7] Ada's ideas were until the 1950s. Since then, Ada has had a programming language named after her. She even has her own holiday in October. This holiday celebrates women who have done amazing things in science, technology, engineering, and mathematics.

Ada chose to live and think outside of the box. She came up with extraordinary ideas that were a century[8] ahead of anyone else's. As a result, she is now known as the "Enchantress of Numbers" and the first computer programmer in history.

GLOSSARY

1. Programmer	A person who writes computer programs.
2. Independent	Not depending on another for livelihood or subsistence.
3. Best of both worlds	A situation in which you can enjoy the advantages of two very different things at the same time.
4. Passionate	Having, showing, or caused by strong feelings or beliefs.

5. Analytical Engine: A proposed mechanical general-purpose computer designed by Charles Babbage.

6. Translate: Express the sense of (words or text) in another language.

7. Revolutionary: Involving or causing a complete or dramatic change.

8. Century: A period of one hundred years.

Muse Museum

More IIG muses
to come...

Ada Lovelace

1815 - 1852

Augusta Ada Byron was born 1815 in England. Her father died when she was only eight years old, and she never had the chance to meet him. He was a famous poet named Lord Byron. Her mother, Lady Byron, wanted Ada to outshine her dad, so she made sure that Ada grew up learning math and science.

Ada met the brilliant and much older inventor Charles Babbage when she was only 17. He was impressed by her creative ideas. They became close friends and spoke about new concepts and inventions. Babbage designed the Analytical Engine – a machine that is now considered the first computer ever imagined.

Nine years later, Ada translated a paper for Babbage that explained what the Analytical Engine was capable of. She added her own notes describing how numbers could be used to tell the machine what to do. Scientists now believe Ada imagined the first computer programming language over 100 years before anyone else.

Ada was only 37 when she died, but her thoughts live on. She has a holiday and a computer language named after her. Her programming theories came a century before the first computer was even built. She is now known as the "Enchantress of Numbers" for her innovative and groundbreaking ideas.

A gallery employee looks at Margaret Carpenter's painting 'Ada Lovelace (1815 -1852) Mathematician; daughter of Lord Byron 1836'

Inspire Deeper

Here at Inspired Inner Genius, we believe that every child is born a genius. Join us in our journey to inspire the world, one child at a time.

Scan the QR code above or visit www.inspiredinnergenius.com/gift

---

Cover designed by Irina Katsimon · Interior designed by Renata Christine · Written by Stephanie Willis · Published by Inspired Inner Genius

Photographic acknowledgement (page 33) A gallery employee looks at Margaret Carpenter's painting 'Ada Lovelace (1815 - 1852) Mathematician; daughter of Lord Byron 1836' c. 2012 © Peter Macdiarmid via Getty Images

Printed in Great Britain
by Amazon

63165398R00020